Beholding Eye

Beholding Eye

Poems by Grace Bauer

CustomWords

Published by CustomWords
P.O. Box 541106
Cincinnati, OH 45254-1106

Typeset in Baskerville by WordTech Communications LLC,
Cincinnati, OH

ISBN: 1933456299
LCCN: 2006927467

Poetry Editor: Kevin Walzer
Business Editor: Lori Jareo

Visit us on the web at www.custom-words.com

Acknowledgments

I would like to thank the editors of the following journals and anthologies in which many of these poems, often in different versions, first appeared:

American Literary Review, Antietam Review, Artemis, Berkeley Poets Cooperative, Birmingham Poetry Review, Black Buzzard Review, The Bridge, Comstock Review, Embers, Gargoyle, Iowa Woman, Iris, Michigan Quarterly Review, Negative Capability, New Orleans Review, Outerbridge, Permafrost, Pinyon Poetry Review, Plainsong, Poet Lore, Poetry, Rattle, Shenandoah, Slipstream, South Dakota Review, South Florida Poetry Review, Southern Poetry Review, Spoon River Poetry Review, Swamproot, Tampa Review, and *Worcester Review.*

"Dancing on the Bar at the Blue Goose Saloon" appeared in *Wherever Home Begins*, Paul B. Janeczko, ed. NY: Orchard Books, 1995

"The Visiting Paleontologist Feels Her Thigh" appeared in *Looking for Your Name: A Collection of Contemporary Poems*, Paul B. Janeczko, ed. NY: Orchard Books, 1993

"Oldies But Goodies" and "She Calms the Savage Beast with Her Aubade" appeared in *Mixed Voices*, Buchwald & Rosten, ed, Minneapolis, MN: Milkweed Editions, 1992

"Her Great Escape" appeared in *Sampler*, Pearl River, NY: Alms House Press, 1992

"Signora Giaconda Tires of Sitting for the Master" appeared in *Mona Poetica*, Decillis & Gillett, ed., Bay City, MI: Mayapple Press, 2005

Lyrics from "She Belongs to Me," by Bob Dylan. Copyright 1965 by Warner Bros., Inc. Copyright renewed by Special Rider Music. International copyright secured. Reprinted by permission.

Some of these poems were first published in the chapbooks, *Where*

You've Seen Her, Pennywhistle Press, Tesuque, NM, 1993, and *Field Guide to the Ineffable: Poems on Marcel Duchamp*, Snail's Pace Press, Cambridge, NY, 1999. My gratitude to Victor Di Suvero, Ken Denberg and Darby Penney.

Thanks also to Jonathan Miles, Katherine Louveau and Toni King for the art tour extraordinaire, and to the University of Nebraska Research Council, the Nebraska Arts Council, and the Kimmel Harding Center for the Arts for their support of my work. And to Kelly Gray Carlisle and Arra Ross for technical assistance.

Cover Art: *Vera's Window* by Ruth Ray (1919-1977), reproduced with permission from the Sheldon Memorial Art Galley and Sculpture Garden and the family of Ruth (Mrs. John Reginald Graham) Ray.

Author Photo: Julia Lauer Cheene

For my family and friends, always.
And in memory of Adam Foote.

Contents

An Epic of the Eyes

She's got everything she needs.
She's an artist. She don't look back.
Bob Dylan

Artemisia Paints the Blood on Judith's Hands

after Artemisia Gentileschi

It's no easy business to paint
a beheading. The muscles in her arms—
they took me days to get right,
to reveal the toughness
of the woman and the task
at hand, articulate the history
written in her face with nearly
imperceptible shadow.

What I wanted was the moment,
the woman captured
in the gesture of freeing
her people, herself, the horror
of what sometimes must be
accomplished, of crimson
disrupting white. I wanted

no rest for the eye
of the viewer, as I had no rest—
obsessed as my subject
with finding a language
for anger that renders
the word mute as Holofernes
the moment after the moment
he recognized death in his own voice.
Silence is a sword
that takes him away
from himself—I sketched it
in her hand like a brush,

labored till my models
nearly wept from exhaustion,
till Rome began to whisper

its nightly melody, and the moon
rose beyond my window, silver
as a coin. Only then could I turn
from the heroine on my easel
to slice myself a bit

of cheese and bread, eating
with the paint still caked
on my fingers, thick and pungent.

In the few hours of dreams
she allows me, I watch
Judith trek the plains
triumphant towards home.
She cradles her terrible trophy
like a child who needs less
than this sleep
she has laid him down for.

Her faithful maid
beside her still trembles
in the afterglow of victory.
Every twig that snaps
beneath their feet could be
his bones breaking, every sigh
of wind a breath his mouth
still gasps for in her arms.

But neither claims regret,
understanding the necessity
of pretense, of using beauty
as a weapon when one must.
They wonder only if they could
have done it quicker, if the line
across his throat might have been more
artfully drawn, or if his heart
might have been a better souvenir
to bear back as testament

of what a woman can do if she must.

But that, my friend, is out
of this painting, which has already
grown larger, more gruesome than I
had pictured it in my mind.
Take her without flinching.
Frame her simply. Promise me
you will hang her in flattering light.

Signora Gioconda Tires of Sitting for the Master

Once, after dinner, my husband
was speaking—of business,
some prediction of weather—I forget—
I was lost in a thought of my own—
but I recall his anger,
how it flared when he saw me
not quite there. He struck me then
and cursed my stupid grin,
yet now he squanders gold to have you
make a likeness of it. Oh, he cares
little for art or me, but he knows
of your renown and desires to possess
a token of it—a well-wrought
adornment to grace his empty wall.

He will approve of the way you have
composed me—the demurely folded
arms, barely visible veils,
the muted tones of my garments—
which will go well with his favorite chair.
The size he'll find convenient,
easy to hang in that perfect niche
where his friends will notice and admire—
will it be me or you?

But the expression you have given me,
I fear that may annoy him. He'll wish
I looked more dignified, closer to his
image of the proper noble's wife.
He'll imagine it's another
of my daydreams that lies behind
the distance in my eyes.
I tell you this to ease the hesitation

that I see in yours, the trembling
in your fingers I noticed when you rearranged
my hair. I think you, too, feel this
portrait may be more that mere commission.

If my husband asks, I will tell him
of the minstrels you employed to entertain
and keep me still, of the pretty boys
who mill about the studio, eager
to satisfy your whims, of the smell
of turpentine and oil that permeates
the rooms, the light that streams through
each window, as if you had drawn it there.
He will never question these stories,
though he will never understand
how little they explain.

He may be astute enough to recognize
that something has been captured here,
but he will never name exactly what it is.
He'll call it—cunning, mystery, bemusement—
let him call it what he will.
His soul, I think, could use a bit of wonder.

So forget about your patron, your boys,
the whole damned world. The peaks
you've sketched in the distance may
exist where love will take us.
Pour some wine, dear Leonardo.
Admit this work is good. Come and lie down
with the legend you have made.

Portraits of the Rich

One can hardly believe their bearing—
posture so regal, one wants to call it
carriage, though motion is rarely implied.
Their faces, composed to inspire
admiration, refuse to give much away.
No museum is complete without a few.

If they are men, their sternness represents
itself as virtue. They stand poised
with a hand hitched in a vest pocket
or finger a shimmering watch fob
to remind us of the value of their time.
Sometimes they sit behind an expanse
of desk, accouterments of their industry
displayed against dark backgrounds.

If women, they are most often dressed
in white. If not white, then blue.
Their pale throats adorned with fine gold chains,
delicate lace framing the hands that lie
clasped in their decorous laps.
On occasion, they demure behind a fan.
One can barely imagine them unclothed
or caught in the act of disrobing.

Such exposure is reserved for the poor
wenches who were paid to serve as models
for the Masters, and who now gaze openly
at us, and those who deemed themselves their betters,
from much better paintings, hung here
on the gallery's equal but opposing walls.

Large Bathers

after Cezanne

Only one figure actually appears
to be *in* the water. The rest lounge
on the banks, the curved lines of their limbs
sketched against what blue it takes
to make the eye see air,
just enough gold ocher to dust
their skin the warmth of summer.

The women are, for the most part, faceless.
Their features crudely drawn, bodies
painted the color of sand—if they are
painted at all. Sometimes untouched
canvas is left to represent bare flesh.

                                    Midpoint
dead-center on the far shore
stands a man washed the color of wheat, fully clothed
beside his wheat-washed pony.

His face, too, is a gap, an absence
of detail we read as visage and longing,
since he, like us, is the voyeur
in this scene, the eye
for whom these bathers are composed.

The village in the distance is hardly more
than a dream, despite the solid cerulean
of its roofs and spire suggesting
civility and containment, which is what
we come to this painting to step out of
for a moment. We enter this idyll to forget
a world that makes us so self-conscious

of our naked selves, we fear
a sight like this might strike us blind.

Mrs. Eakins' Final Touches

after Susan Macdowell Eakins

First your student, then your wife, then your model.
In becoming these I slowly had
to unbecome myself. I was transformed
into another of your finely-rendered subjects,
a life-like figure you'd composed in enigmatic light.

Oh, I know you loved me deeply and bragged
to others often that your Susie had an eye
for color finer than your own, but you had a way
of needing that, too often, overwhelmed me.
I defended you from all those fools
who thought your work too bold.

I do miss you, Tom. Your passion, wit. The wild determination
that you brought to life and art—but I must admit this solitude
your sudden passing left me in some days feels like luxury.
The joy of work's a pleasure I denied myself too long.

What I love best, ironically, is painting images of you.
Your face. Your hands. Your body. Which I resurrect
upon my easel now. It took me years but, dear,
I think I've finally captured your true likeness.

Life-like. Silent. Staring from the shadows
that I paint you in. Thomas, my love,
you taught me. But not everything I know.

Frida Digresses on Red

after Frida Kahlo

Rojo, we say in my language,
which captures more precisely
its vehemence, the violence
and pleasure it catches in the eye.
The word demands we force
out breath—not unlike, say
Jesus, who knew the color well;
who was, perhaps, God's metaphor
for what is *rojo* in us all.

In this painting it draws you
to my shawl, offering
warmth against cool blues,
and yet, a sense of danger.
Here it spatters pain
across the canvas; here it blooms—
tiny *flamboyants* in my hair;
There it flashes in the parrot's
wings, and here it is life itself,
ending before it begins.

How I wanted to beget
that life! What pictures
I could have made for a child!
Not grand like my love's—
who moves whole walls
with his sermons—but visions
in their own right moving.
Parts of my self scraped
with a palette knife, laid on
thicker than blood.

Rojo! To your ear it sounds
close to a laugh, but there is
nothing funny about it. Not in these
matters of life and death, these paintings
that are more me than mine.

Room in New York

after Edward Hopper

Note how many rectangles and squares:
the window we view the couple through,
the three black lines we read
as shutters, three indistinct pictures
that hang on the flamboyant green walls,
the old black upright she pings upon
with a single index finger.
Note how the red of her dress repeats
the lamp and chair, how the stark white
of his shirt echoes the sheet
of what is meant to represent music—
although it is, most curiously, blank.

It is only the figures themselves
who appear to have nothing in common.
Not just that he is absorbed in his paper—
because who among us has not been so
eager to learn the news of the world
that we've allowed ourselves to get lost
in print. But look
                    how she sits at that piano.
Not facing it, as someone intent on playing would.
No, she sits as if she means to face him,
but has turned to the keys as an afterthought,
a way to entertain herself while she waits
to catch his eye, as she has ours.

Her pale skin is almost ghostly.
The bow on her shoulder
an odd attempt at adornment
like the dead center doily that protects
(*why, oh why*, we might ask like Miss Bishop)
the small brown table he's leaning towards from nothing.

I imagine her sounding out middle C,
perhaps hitting a sharp for emphasis.
I imagine the piano itself is hopelessly
out of tune, and that both of them have been
waiting their whole lives for attention—
each other's or anyone's—or a song to take them
somewhere beyond the confines of the space they are in.

But his stocks have gone down or his team
may be up for the pennant, and she has
her club or some project to type for the boss.
The city outside is all menace and promise,
all streetlight and exhaust.
We ourselves could, at any moment,
climb a fire escape, pick a lock, break down
the brown of that door, and be inside
there with them, like them—beside ourselves,
bored to distraction, without a word to say.

After Breakfast in Fur

But if you speak your own language
that nobody understands yet,
you may have to wait a long time
before you hear an echo.
                              Meret Oppenheim

Monsieur Madame
  Bon apetit   a bit
          of the fantastic

a bite of
  dream
          to help you
start your day
  a banquet
          you can eat
with your fingers
  swallow
          through your eyes
alone this cup will
  always runneth
          over   this plate
will lick you
  clean   curl up
          in the curve

of this spoon
  and rest your
          head along
the handle
  till time's disembodied
          hands announce
the nightmares we promise

to serve you
        for dessert

Louise Invites You to Her Sky Cathedral

What would you do with your life
if you didn't risk it?
                    Louise Nevelson

It is not black
It is not wood
It is not sculpture

It is between
and beyond all
these and I

am the architect
of shadow
the scavenger

who translates
the junk of other
lives into a celestial

banquet for the eye
which is—if you will
only see it—in its own

constant awareness
mapping the physical into
a geography of being

identification is love
love is recognition
art is anywhere

you put into perspective
enter with an open
mind into this enclosure

you can move an inch
and circle the world

Birthday

after Dorothea Tanning

She seems to be asking something of me,
this bare-breasted woman standing bare-foot
in her house made of doors—each one
opalescent and opening onto another,
and another, until coming and going
become more or less the same thing.

She looks unfazed by all the options.
Her green gaze focused far-off, beyond
any destination I can envision
outside the frame. The hue of her eyes
is echoed in what appears, at first glance,
to be seaweed draping from her waist,
but on closer inspection reveals
a tangled garland of women's bodies,
contorted like the damned in Rodin's
Gates of Hell. She wears them well,
looks both elegant and disheveled,
festooned in purple, green and gold
like a refugee from some solitary Carnival.

And then there's the creature at her feet:
lamb-faced, rat-tailed, monkey-clawed
and eagle-winged—an animus caught
between *animosity* and *amour* who looks
as if he has just landed or has, perhaps,
been waiting patiently for her
to give a command. He's a guide
any woman might be tempted to follow herself
if the time were right. And time, I think, may be

what this painting is all about—
if paintings are really *about* any thing.

Time, which takes its toll on us and composes
all our entrances and exits. Time, which we must learn
to celebrate even as we watch it pass,
with no answers as to where it might take us,
what doors it might open for us
as we get closer, and then too close to close.

Georgia, at Ninety, Learns to Make a Vessel

after Georgia O'Keeffe

Since that day I wasted
an hour searching
for a tube of blue
to edge a bone,
I have known my years
of making color speak
what I can find
no human words for
had come full circle, back
to a black line on white.

For weeks then, I walked
the Faraway, not sad
exactly, certainly not
in despair, but in wonder
of the solid shapes
I could still discern
in shadows.

It made me think
of Stieglitz, for whom
beauty lay in gradations
of light. He could rave
for days about silver
tones, the clarity of grays.

Finally I realized my eyes
were not so much *failing*,
simply learning the art
of revision as I had
never understood it before.

My hands always did have

a mind of their own. To see
with them now is simply
another lesson in perspective.

I roll and coil and roll
and coil and smooth
away the rough spots,
cup my palms around
the clay till I hear it
sing for glaze.

And if I fail, the object
is still useful.
It stands filling space
in its beautiful way.
And it pleases me
to fire this earth
that holds both air and water.

Imogen Composes Mr. Roethke

The formula for doing a good job
in photography is to think like a poet.
                    Imogen Cunningham

I have photographed everything light
falls on, but it has always been human
faces I love to shoot the best.
With a face there's little chance
of duplication. Each one's unique
and suggests another story.
Another glimpse of what it means
to be alive in the visible world.

Ted was such a monumental man,
awkward in his immensity. I recognized
at once the familiar look of someone
who has journeyed from the edge of
a language he's lived in completely
without ever naming home.

On the sofa, in the garden, he hunkered
like a caged bear, displayed against his will
in the available light of day. I sensed
he'd be more comfortable in shadow,
a landscape where he could take root
and blossom quietly into himself.

I think he liked the way I disappeared
his body into background and
allowed his naked head alone to reveal
the furious beauty of its flaws.
My image of him looks about
to voice a question no one asks,
the one a man like him constantly
answers in the silent epic of his eyes.

The Eye of the Beholder

after Diane Arbus

All human beauty is
an aberration, a mirror
trick drawing us
into itself. Into what is not.

And what is desire? A lack
invented by belief,
a return to the thrill
of the unfamiliar we recognize
in an instant as ourselves.

I know this in sight.
In the click of a shutter
revealing the barely real.
Strip glamour of its thin
veneer and you find something
raw. Elegant. You find the part
in us we're all afraid of
staring straight in the face.

But I can't turn my back
or blink. I feel myself
connecting through captured light
to a darkness that beckons, a darkness
much less frightening than you fear.

My subjects appear calm
because they are. They compose
themselves before my lens
like hallucinations we have
all shared, metaphors that suspend
us between what we want
to be and what we become.

Try to picture yourself
beyond denial. Run your hands
across your average face,
your normal body. And tell me
how you differ from these
miracles that always make you
want to look away.

His Light Meters. Her Dark Rooms.

I: The Photographer Explains His Poor Exposure

The problem with the photo
is I left my shutter
too wide open for too long,
absorbed too much
surrounding light.
Her image got lost in the glare.

I should have realized
from the contact sheets
all the fixer in the world
would never capture what I had
seen clearly, but I tried
to develop it, over and over,
hoping I could make her
come out of the negative.

II: The Man Behind Her Picture

He labors through the night
in the tiny room that guarantees
the darkness he needs

enlarging gestures
she never would have
noticed, cropping what he calls
distracting details
to compose her
into perfect still life.

But her best moments
are more cinematic.
Each one flashes by

so rapidly, she appears
to be going somewhere.

3: Alone in the Gallery

She is the only mobile figure
in the room, framed
by faces staring from the walls.

The lighting is bad.
She must side-step
each portrait to avoid
seeing her own features
reflected in the glass.

As she walks from print
to print, she imagines
still eyes imagining her
caught in a moment and framed
in an empty room.

4: Seeing Herself in the Show

It could be anyone's shoulder.
But he points out the particulars
of hair, chin, breasts—
angles and arcs he found
worth attention, if only for the shadows
they happened to cast at the time.

Though there is little beauty
in the subject, as object
she forms a composition of interest.
Anonymous in the beholder's eye.
A lovely lie of light.

Field Guide to the Ineffable:
Poems on Marcel Duchamp

Words find their real meaning and their real place in poetry.
Marcel Duchamp

I was looking to see if I could make Marcel out of it but I can't.
Gertrude Stein

Descending Nude

She'll never shimmer for me
     again as she did
        when I was seven, maybe eight

(old enough to read
     the word *descending*, old
        enough to know *nude*

meant she wasn't wearing
     any clothes) & stood here
        in this very room, calmly watching

as she walked out of the canvas.
     She didn't clank, as I might
        have expected, but rather

sauntered silently into the space
     that had been mine, crossing
        a line I had not known was there.

As I recall I wasn't at all
     surprised (which seems surprising
        to me now) simply intrigued

by how all those angles &
     a few words could make her
        come alive in what I saw

as the actual world. My mom & dad
     were across the room somewhere
        maybe scratching their heads

over the urinal. My brother sulked
     in a corner, pissed that we'd come here
        instead of the Franklin Institute

down the street, where he longed
   to walk through the heart yet again
      & hear its insistent throb.

I see now I had already chosen art
   above science, though this was years
      before I myself turned to words

or saw the world this way again
   through windowpane. Years before
      my brother began to self-destruct

searching for escape or vision,
   & my parents turned gray. Today
      the nude appears armored & static

& though her muted tones of browns
   & golds glow lovely in the light,
      she stays within the confines

of her frame. I see, in fact, she isn't
   a woman at all, but a machine
      designed to disrobe the viewer

an idea intended to change
   forever how we see.

Marcel Dreams a Match with Paul Cezanne

Naturally, he suggests cards
but I insist on *my* game

& set up a board that grows
larger than us both; the colors

of the rank & file shift
subtly as we line up our pieces.

This will be, I know, a game of mind
& winning will matter little.

It will be observation that counts
in the end. If there is one.

How can I begin to check
the man who revised the act

of seeing in my time? A man who sang small
& yet became, in his own time, a mountain.

He moves his pawns distractedly, leaving more
than one knight vulnerable to capture. I expose

my queen until she looks like one of his
bathers lounging in blue air, and my king poses, nude

& still as an apple. Immovable, yet ready to fall.
My opponent will not take advantage.

Nor will he readily yield. I know I will
eventually concede to the play of light.

But for the moment, the joy is pondering.
It's the moves we do not make that move us most.

Readymade #1: Un Chanson/On Chance

Works which are not works of art, which was
a dream that became unnecessary, revealing
the unexpressed but intended & the unintentionally expressed.
Now I am drawing on chance alone, conducting
an absence of investigation which allows
everyone to be for himself, as in a shipwreck
locked inside this cage outside the world.
To live is to believe, that's my belief.
The bachelor grinds his chocolate himself
in silence, slowness, solitude, and I
am making my way toward beatitude.
The genius of the modern world is in machinery.
It's something other than yes, no, and indifferent.
Rrose Sélavy and I avoid The Eskimos of exquisite words.

Marcel & Me at the Horn & Hardart

The way to most men's hearts
may be through their stomachs,
Rrose Sélavy once said to me,
but the way to Marcel's mind
is through the eye.

Amazed now by the automat, he declares
he wants to eat everything he sees:

the precisely cut triangles
of ham & tuna sandwiches
of bologna & pimento spread:

the perfect round scoops
of potato salad & cole slaw
of macaroni & cheese:

the thick sweet wedges
of cake called
devil's & angel's food:

the sticky crumbling spades
of apple & pecan pie
& crystalline-colored cubes
of jello composed
in clear glass bowls:

all of it delectably framed
behind little locked doors
that let us peer in at hunger,
that let us open them
if we have exact change.

Rrose Sélavy would salivate,
he says, surveying
this exhibition of edibles.

This is what he loves about America.
And he loves it more than Joe McCarthy.
More, he thinks, even than art
(because to him, it all could be).

Marcel & Man Ray Play Tennis

Lovely as the fortuitous encounter
on a dissecting table of a sewing machine
and an umbrella
                Man Ray

no court
no net
no tramlines
    to confine us

no language
    beyond *yes*
and both of us
    eager to serve

any point of contact
    is a sweetspot
every volley
    a kill

we create
    our own rules
as we go along
    and break them
as soon as we can

unconcerned
    with faults and lets
always playing hard
    though it is more
    (and less perhaps)
than a game

a perpetual motif
    of changing ends

and ending changes
   in our eyes
all returns are good

each set lasts
   a lifetime &
the match ends
   inevitably
in love

Sisters: Simultaneous

They face each other
& they turn away
staring into time
& beyond it

Yvonne & Magdaleine
torn between their own
adolescence & age
tattered in the space
that divides & joins
their chiseled profiles
as the cascades of their
chestnut-colored curls
take on a life of their own

These little sisters portrayed
in twisted perspective & time:
contiguous & convergent
discountenanced & discomposed
so I can see depth lying
on the surface of the picture plane

and remember
when I walk away
their singular sad eyes
that appear to be looking
inward & yet at me

at us all

Rrose Sélavy No Longer Sings *La Vie En Rose*

How many years can a woman pose for a man
in the same bad hat & ratty fur
before the world goes gray before her eyes
and even *la-de-la-de-la-de-la* sounds like the blues?

How many nights can she lie alone while
the avant guard goes galloping toward the future
on their hobbyhorse? I tell you, my heart may belong
to da-da, but even an alter ego needs l'amour

which is more than a mere word and goes beyond mechanics.
Love—so easy to make, yet more difficult to create
by far than art. That's why some people call
this kind of song a torch. And I keep singing—
la-de-la—to make something burn.

Song for the Sad Young Man

When the young man came back home
When the young man came back home
He poked his nose in his fine soul's frame
                                   Jules Laforgue

Call me sentimental, Marcel
but I knew he was you
at first glance

I knew he was you
clattering & collatering
along a long long line
of tracks I could picture
outside the frame

I knew it was you
dislocating yourself
while staying stationary,
not allowing the figure
you'd made to get off
at any stop

It was you, I knew
behind the dapper disguise
of a Sherlock Holmes-like pipe
& a hat (I swear I see a hat)
more fashionable than the cloche
you posed on Rrose

I knew he was you
having a tryst with *triste*
& I knew his sadness
was true, though later you
claimed it just a word

It was & is you
on your way toward a home
that never held you,
you, crossing that line
that represents time
& in no time at all
you have arrived

Readymade #2: Fat Chance

my capital is time/the Ministry of Coincidences/the interrogation of shop windows/in the infinitive/when you tap something you don't always recognize the sound/always there has been the necessity for circles in my life/a mechanized mind against a machine/a little game between I & me/one must occupy this delight /I don't want to destroy art for anyone but myself/there is no solution because there is no problem/the image that rises out of revery/the main thing is to die without knowing it/all chess players are artists/I'm a pseudo/a delay in glass

Me & Marcel at the Five & Dime

He wants to sign his name
   to the notions' counter
   where the pale sales girl
   doesn't have a clue
   who he is & he
   likes it that way.

To the housewares department
   where the ruddy clerk
   looks lost amidst
   the enamel & chrome
   of appliances only
   housewives appreciate.

To the lingerie display
   where a line-up of legs
   sport hose in various shades
   of beige & the disarmed
   mannikin's torso is imprisoned
   in a white brassiere.

To the make-up counter
   where Tangee Lipstick looms
   a lurid orange & Evening in Paris
   reeks inside its cobalt bottles
   next to hair removers & vanishing creams.

To the lunch counter
   where blue-plate specials
   & day-old coffee grow
   colder by the minute.

To the children's department.
To the hardware division.
To outdoor & gardening supplies:

So much readymade stuff
  made to make us
  want it, though little
  these days can be had
  for pocket change.

*'Ow much do you sink
Monsieur Woolworth iz worth?*

One helluva lotta wool,
  I guarantee ya.
A buffalo herd a nickels,
  you can betchur ass.
Marcel whips out a cheap
  Flare pen & scrawls
  Duchamp across it all.

Silver jingles
  in the pockets
  of the world.

The Joke on *La Joconde*

No matter how long or often
I look (*L.H.O.O.Q? L.H.O.O.Q!*)
trying to keep my eyes   open
to revision   it is still
always a woman   I see:

Leonardo's legendary Lady
of the Louvre   Lady of the Enigmatic
Smirk & Sentimental Song
Lady of the Tourists
Must-See: A-R-T: But lady
nonetheless   or rather   woman.

No Dali-like mustache   (waxed?)
No graffitied goatee   (pencil strokes
from the champ   of camp)
No tall or tantalizing tale   re-titling:
(*elle a chaud au cul*) may imply
can drag (up?   down?)
this piece of the old master or
re-member her   manly in my mind.

No man's hand   not, even, Marcel's
can sunder what another's
painted into   (on?)
that face that defies   defacement—

though I must admit
(*Look! L.H.O.O.Q.?*) the background
always draws my gaze into
the fiction of distance   behind her.

It's the hands: Hands of a her:
those long tapered fingers
gone unsung   (though so demurely posed

and finely rendered)   that make me
keep seeing her as   (soft touch):   her:
and female to the bone.

Marcel Duchamp Does Lunch with Andy Warhol: A Film Script for the Blink of an Eye

(Scene: A vast warehouse space filled with a few scattered couches and chairs. Tables everywhere, most of them cluttered with art supplies and work in-progress. In the foreground, a low wide wall made of Campbell soup cans, which Warhol (standing) slowly dis-assembles, methodically opening one after another with an electric can opener that whines obnoxiously. He lines the opened cans up on a table that is otherwise bare. Warhol is dressed completely in black. Duchamp, dressed in a rumpled tweed coat, sits in an overstuffed chair and watches Warhol. He says nothing, but smokes a pipe throughout and occasionally nods his head enthusiastically, as if in approval. In the corner stands an anonymous woman, nude, except for a video camera, which she uses to tape the action).

Warhol: Soup. Would you like some soup? Here, have some soup. I've got plenty. I love this soup. It's American. Red, white, and gold labeled cans. And you can pour it from the can right into a pan or even put the can itself on the stove without the label if you're in a pinch. Which I have been. You can add a little water. You can add a little milk. Go gourmet and add some pepper and a little parsley. Or not. Anyway you go, you got soup. And it's quick and it's easy and I like the color a lot. But then, I tend to like things. Especially soup. It stores so well. Even after you take it out of the store. It'd keep forever. Probably even if they dropped the big one. Which they already did. You could stack up a wall of soup in a shelter and wait for the next mushroom cloud. Which will come sooner or later. Stacked soup. It even sounds good. What more can a man ask for? Except maybe a sandwich on the side. One made from Wonderbread. And maybe some Spam. Soup and something on the side. And you got yourself lunch. You got yourself dinner. You got yourself a snack. And then, maybe afterwards, a leisurely half-hour smoking a good Dutch Master.

Marcel applauds appreciatively, laughing.

Anonymous Woman: Cut.

The End

The Bride Not Even, Nor Her Bachelors Bare

To tell the truth
I would see   no bride
I would see   no bachelors
if not for the words
that tell me   they are there.

I look at & into & beyond
the Large Glass to
the far wall
      (from one side)
or out
      (from the other)
to another glass
      (this one a window)
& to the fountain
in the courtyard   outside

beyond which once stood   a stone
woman   made by a woman
(I have read)   you
once may have loved.

Now there's a lot
full of cars   that look about
as amorous as these
mechanical lovers   who

never quite made it
out of your mind
where they reside   still
definitively incomplete
& untouchable. Untouching.

To tell the truth   what I love best
is the way sun glints

off the accidental—
                          those cracks
    & shards   by which both
bride & bachelors were   almost
                          (even)
but not quite   undone.

Readymade #3: Drawing on Chance

the unexpressed but intended   I don't want
to destroy art for anyone but myself   a little game
between I & me   everyone for himself
as in a shipwreck   something other than
yes, no & indifferent   a mechanized mind
against a machine   to live is
to believe, that's my belief   always there has
been the need for circles in my life   one must occupy
this delight   there is no
solution because there is no problem   my way toward
beatitude   the bachelor grinds
his chocolate himself   works which are
not works of art   this cage outside
the wor(l)d

Marcel Meets Georgia at 291

What do you see
   in these skyline lights?

The fragrance of motion
   in a Manhattan night.

And do you sense anything
   in these cliffs? This sky?

I hear you seeing
   through my eyes.

And what do you hear
   in this hue of blue?

Something luminous
   that might be true.

And what of these flowers
   made larger than life.

They bloom like a virgin
   on the verge of wife.

And what in my work
   speaks most to your own?

The bones. The bones.
   The bones. The bones.

Given: More than Water & Gas

She *must* be alive.
How else could she keep
the lamp held aloft
like an X-rated Miss Liberty?

But let's face it,
it could be otherwise.
Let's face it, he kept her
face out of sight by design.

Even if we gouged out
the peep holes we're invited
to spy on her through,
even if we broke down the doors,
we might find he made this
ready maid without giving her
a head at all beyond that hint
of blond hair that hangs
across her right shoulder.

Let's face it, it's the gash
between her legs he wanted
us to look at, that cut
in the fabricated flesh
that bears little resemblance
to the well-known secret
a real woman might choose to display.

The postcard pretty
background of kodachrome trees
& mechanical trick of light
that makes the waterfall
appear to really flow,
he had to know they would not
distract our gaze for long.

Our eye is drawn, as he knew
it would be, to the forbidden
arrayed and splayed in harsh illumination—
a garish glare that exposes so much
while revealing very little.

Me, Marcel, Rrose & the Buddha

1

Marcel at midnight
in either Paris or New York
is outside the field
of vision, walking
in a lemony light that glows
from a ready-made moon.

2

A rrose is not always
a rose is a Rrose
& by any other name
smells sweeter, even.

3

What do we see
when we realize
our eyes
are not our own?

4

Somewhere between
yes & no, Marcel
makes an image rise
out of revery.

5

Life is an accident
bound to happen.
Death, a rendezvous.

6

A Seller of Salt
named Richard Mutt
mistook our Rrose

for a simple slut.

But Miss Sélavy
brought Mutt to his knees.
He discovered she stands
just like him when she pees.

7
The box is packed
in the valise
& we are ready
to travel nowhere
& perhaps

8
When Marcel claimed
breathing as his
main occupation, he was
speaking for us all.

9
The boddhisatva
Rrose Sélavy sits
sipping rosehip tea.

10
Now even in
the Sicíeté Anonyme
everyone knows
your names.

11
In the end, all of us
breed our necessary
quota of dust.

12
Seeing the Buddha

on the bathroom wall,
we recognize the landscape
of his face as our own.

13
As for me, I know
perhaps nothing
beyond what I saw
as a child.

Where You've Seen Her

A woman like that is misunderstood.
I have been her kind.
Anne Sexton

Where You've Seen Her

after Cindy Sherman

Perhaps you caught her gazing
   at her image in a mirror, or staring
out a window into a distance you thought
   might be yours. Perhaps you saw yourself
in her eyes.

Perhaps it was in moonlight or starlight,
   or the blue haze of a TV screen or
the smoke of a seedy bar where the glow
   from her cigarette gathered the night
around, or perhaps it was in sunlight
   so bright

you had to squint. It hurt
   your eyes. Maybe you've never seen
her at all, or so often you have long
   since forgotten to look, allowing
memory or expectation to make what you think
   she is real.

Perhaps you've brushed by her
   in a subway, at a close-out sale,
in some library where she reached
   for the very book you wanted to read;
or maybe in a dream she cruised by
   in a red

sedan, on a black mare, saying something
   you couldn't quite fit your voice
around but desperately needed to say.
   She could be your mother, your sister,
your favorite or most hated aunt,
   the girl

next door, the one you left
    behind, who got away, the woman too
good or not good enough for you, the one
    who never knew you existed, who's been
waiting for you all her life, the one
    you've been

mistaken for. Perhaps you gave her
    your ring, took her cherry, paid
for her lunch, lent her cab fare
    or lipstick, voted her *Snow Queen*
or *Most Congenial*. You might have
    given her

flowers, advice, or hell,
    a lift to the nearest phone booth,
the time of day. You might have opened
    doors for her, or old wounds,
maybe you held her or wished you could
    hold her

or be her or never had been.
    She is always more or less
than you imagined or would have
    her be. She is the stranger you
always recognize. More than shadow
    less than

substance, not quite yours or her own.
    Since she has never really been
there, you know that she can never
    go away.

Morning Becomes Her Henry

She is thumbing the *Dreamsongs*
at three a.m. alarmed
by a silence that keeps her
from falling asleep.
She has no wine, no cigarettes.
No inner resources left.

Lighting fire for water,
she brews some camomile.
Lust and loneliness clench
two fists in the pockets of her
robe as she paces the kitchen.
Even her bones feel bored.

When the kettle whistles, she
is startled into a tension, watching
a woman she never wanted
to know lift a steaming cup
in two hands, settling
for the only warmth she's bound to
get before sunrise.

She Calms the Savage Beast with Her Aubade

Still exhausted at dawn, she plays
Vivaldi, Muddy Waters,
a little Grateful Dead.
She talks to the black rose,
her wandering jew,
her ailing aloe that's yellowed
and rotting from too much attention.

She pinches bits of dill and thyme
for eggs, then remembers
she has none, but she knows
common hunger is not very hard to ignore.

Outside, a wind chime clangs
against a drain pipe, a prism throws
color dancing across white walls.

And the birds, more hungry
than she'll ever feel, peck
the frozen ground before breaking
into what we're used to
calling songs.

Her New Birds

All winter she has watched
them through the window:
one red-breasted woodpecker
two tufted titmice, half a dozen
mourning doves and more

slate-colored junkos than she ever
managed to count. Not to mention
a varied slew of sparrows, the jays
who got so fat and comfortable
they took to preening on the porch

not bothering to retreat
when she got close. She liked to think
she'd earned their trust, maybe
even friendship, but today they're gone
and a flock of strange starlings

run rampant on the grass, bold
enough to attack a lone
squirrel, who has come, she supposes,
out of his seasonal hiding.
They squawk at her as she approaches

with fresh seed, as if to warn
her away from what's theirs.
Ungrateful, she thinks, *they'd bite
the hand that feeds them.*
Still, she does. Hoping

the sun that catches
rainbows on their stark
wings signals spring will soon
be coming—no matter what else
may be forced to leave.

Before the Storm

September's been a flurry
of birds going
somewhere she's not.
A sky undecided
between shades of gray.

She points out starlings
to a stranger on the bus,
giving him a name
for the startle of wings
ascending from beneath
the Coolidge Bridge.

She tells him this *Gloria*
won't amount to much,
not sure where her certainty
comes from. Lord knows,
she'd welcome something
decisive as a tragedy of weather.

. . . . .

Next day, she sleeps
through her predictions, wakes
to the bossy cackle of jays.
Light from a crack
in the clouds falls flat.
The blue of Magritte.

Outside the neighbors clear
what little debris the wind
scattered, empty the emergency
buckets of water they'd stored.
Strip tape from the windows.

There's an air of disappointment
in their chatter. How relieved
they say they are. For once
she can claim she was right to prepare
herself for nothing, knowing nothing
will follow this calm.

Her Search for Great Causes

Undue Sexual Desire - Causes:
Excessive eating of all stimulating foods
such as eggs, meats of all kinds, cheese,
chocolate, tea, coffee and all alcoholic
drinks. . . (novel reading and impure thoughts
are also great causes)
                    Jethro Kloss

The weather doesn't help much.
Humidity lays its sticky hands
on every inch of skin.
Even the slight stir of breeze
comes like hot breath
down her neck.

She lies half nude
before an open window
running her tongue around the rim
of a frosted glass of bourbon.
She eats oysters—raw
with extra Tabasco,
scrapes buttered artichokes
between her perfect white teeth.

Scattered across the rumpled sheets
are D.H. Lawrence, Henry Miller,
Faulkner, a few trashy Gothics.
She has been through the tryst
in the hallway, the corn crib,
that gardener in the grass.
She will wait all of August
for the dark and brooding man.
Perhaps a demon, perhaps a wayward heir.
He will sneak up her

stairs in the moonlight
and make her blood run cold.

Conundrum

She could never really see herself
the way he said he saw her:
not the sultry smile
in Leonardo's painting,
not the wicked Ariel
in his poem.

He had himself
convinced the other woman
he wanted, wanted her.
That woman wanted him.
And she wanted a man
who was crazy and distant,
and even more afraid than her
of wanting anything.

And she wanted him
to convince her it all comes
down to passion;
that the heart is nothing
but a hollow pump
designed to keep the flesh warm,
just one tough muscle
that can wear thin or give out
but never really break.

Art Like Love

She is taking him
at his words.
Pushed to their rough
edges, she leaps
before she looks
into meaning.

Sometimes rhythm
is its own reward.
Sometimes an image
barely glimpsed
is what memory holds
longest.

When she comes
across a perfect line
she lets him take her
inside his poem.

Like a man
inside a woman can
take her
outside of herself.

Her Red Dress

Stepping still wet
from love into the shower,
still wet from
the shower into his robe,
she left it hanging innocently
on a wooden peg behind
his bedroom door, where it was

discovered by a woman
she didn't know would be there.
A woman who didn't know.
And suddenly it screamed,
shocking as Bette Davis
in *Jezebel*, surrounded
by a waltz of virginal lace
and demurely downcast eyes.

It became a sign demanding STOP!
And something did.
Not just them, but something
in her that once opened easily.
Like a flower. Like a book.

Some nights she dreams
she's in a forest, lost
and looking—though she's never
sure what for. She turns
a corner—if you can
call it that—and suddenly
the trees are thickly draped
like bayou oaks in Spanish moss.
Only what hangs in that heat
is every dress she has ever owned.
Every dress she has
ever taken off for a man.

Her Great Escape

Romance pulls in
to her driveway in a gray car.
Their hands reach for warmth
across the gear shift
as they talk themselves deeper
into the desire they are
trying to talk themselves out of.

The moon's a white slice
in a black sky, like the moons
that tip their twined fingers,
like the Cheshire cat's
half-assed smile,
like all the cheesy similes
she has heard the moon be like.

She'd hand over her credit cards
if she thought he'd drive her
anywhere but crazy.
Pay for all the gas.
But what he's offering is temperate
as the climate, unreliable as the moon
reflected on the trunk of the old Nova
that's parked down the block.

Smooth as Sam Cooke
singing *You Send Me* on the radio,
she bows out on the last refrain
and leaves what might be
possible, idling in the dark.

Oldies But Goodies

Because she's had more than her share
of sad stories and Molson's Ale,
she finds herself at midnight
circling the City of Brotherly Love
singing her heart out with the girl groups
playing on the radio.

The Chiffons do *One Fine Day*
like it's still 1963
and all the boys she dreamed
she'd fall in love with weren't dead
or gay or still strung out from Nam,
drinking off a rough divorce or looking
for a wife they think will look good
on their resumes.

To the fast-talking DJ
this is just a good night's work,
but he's doing a job on her.
Her head spins like a worn-out 45,
back to when she'd bump and grind
all night to The Temptations or The Miracles,
before she realized lost love
was worse than any lyric, when she still
wondered what the Kingsmen
really sang in *Louie, Louie.*

Her Black Slip

Her favorite color
and the color he
most liked to watch
her slip out of

sometimes barely
getting in the front
door before they would
wrestle each other

to the bed or floor
crazy with wanting
whatever they gave
or took from each other

maybe just plain crazy
she wears that color
now like a nun
or a widow in mourning
sane and sober

still a bit dramatic
in the right light
she wears that color
and it's still her favorite

although she cannot
say the same for him.

She Marvels at His Face

which appears in dreams still
so clear after all these years—
clearer than the sky which,
this morning, is lost
in a haze; clearer than the face
of the man who, last night
in the pale blue light of a bar,
mistook her for a woman he claimed
he once knew in Chicago.
He seemed so sure and happy,
she thought she might be
better off as that woman
who could inspire so much delight
by a chance reappearance.
For a moment, the wind and blues
of a city she'd never even seen
became her past, till her midwestern
friend turned back to his bourbon
and said, *No, I guess you're too tall
and too young, and it's better
you're not her after all these years.*
She repeats the words: *after all these years* . . .
as if it were the first time she'd heard them,
and wonders why *these* is so important,
why *these* negates all the years
that came before, when the face
that might have been hers
in a bar or his in a dream
was a sight beyond question—
too familiar to notice, too constant
to miss or imagine ever gone.
She thinks maybe memory has it all
wrong—his lips were thinner,
his eyes a duller brown
and she's really smaller

than she appears. Still a girl
despite time. After all,
these years have a way
of deceiving us with the burden
of whatever we have gained in them,
the blindness of all we've lost.

On LSD at Sunset Pier She Thinks
of Wallace Stevens

The orange sunshine drops
through purple haze
into the ocean.
She joins tonight's crowd
in applause.

Sufis dance.
Krishnas chant.
Second-rate musicians
play too loud.
A queen sways by
with a silver tray, singing
Don't be shy! Buy my pie!
Take a look at my tasty tarts!

A blue-haired lady on a bike
wheels her poodle around in a basket.
The poodle, in a tartan sweater,
stands on hind legs and points
a little hard-on into the wind.
The mime falls from her invisible ladder.
The juggler drops his balls.

There is no idea of order
here in Key West.
This is all for money and madness.
Anyone singing is singing
for joy or spare change.

The Visiting Paleontologist Feels Her Thigh

Home, he is known
as a shy man, given
to minute analysis and quiet
evenings with his family in the den,
but here he is taken
with the role attention gives him.

She hangs on every word
when he lectures about his digs
in the desert, his theories
of where we have come from,
how far gone some things are.

Afterwards, there are questions
and cocktails. He has too many
of both and by the time
she extends her hand in a simple
greeting, he takes
the gesture for much more
than it's meant, clings to her
slender fingers as if they were
a link he had just uncovered.

He notes the delicate slope
of her cheekbones, the firm
square set of her jaw, but misses
the flash of annoyance
in her eyes when he runs his free hand
down the curve of her spine
and lets it come to rest on
her hipbone as if it belonged.

She clears her throat, retreats
across the room to her lover
and wraps her arm around his waist,

hoping this evidence will convince
the man of science she knows
where true affection lies.
He observes the obvious
clues and blushes, then strikes up
a conversation on the Pleistocene
with a colleague who's eager to please,
and rambles on till the party's over
and she has left without speaking.
By tomorrow, he'll bury the memory
of his embarrassment and her name.
But tonight he sleeps in a stranger's bed
and dreams about the flesh that hides her bones.

Her Steady Date with Sorrow

He shows up like clockwork
for three meals a day, makes her late
for every bus, distracts her on the job.

She comes home to find him drinking
her wine, smoking her last
cigarette, lounging with his boots
propped up on her coffee table.

Oh, he's cocky! He makes himself
right at home. Nights he slides into bed
between her and her sweetest lovers.

She goes out on the town, trying hard
to lose him, but just as the best looking
man at the bar steps up to ask her
what she's drinking, there's sorrow

that sly devil, peering over his shoulder
and winking to beat the band. After years
of this, she's grown accustomed to him.

At least, she thinks, she'll never lack company.
He's loyal. Consistent. He laughs
at her worst jokes, revises her best lines.

She can count on that bastard.
She knows he'll always be there
whether she needs him or not.

It Ain't Love, It's Just Country and Western

Darlin', punch another waltz
into that jukebox. The dance floor's
half as big as Texas, and she feels
warm as Abilene in August
when she's in your arms.

Don't bother with that tune
about how you were born to ramble.
The beat's too fast to dance to
and the song's been played so often
the damn record's scratched and warped.

If your first love is a pick-up truck,
a horse or a guitar,
hell, she won't care!
If gambling is your game, well then
tomorrow you can call this hand
a bust and hit the road.

But tonight the moon is nearly full
and a few appropriate stars
demand that she feel *something*.
Call it tenderness.
Call it passion.
Either one is worth at least your quarter.

So play another slow song
on that jukebox. Buy the girl
a beer. You can waltz her
across that dance floor
like it's Texas, and kiss her
inside the elbow, just like
your daddy told you to.

Dancing on the Bar at the Blue Goose Saloon

She has stumbled tonight
from bar to bar, settling here
for the pool, the choice
of tunes on the Wurlitzer
that starts on a kick.

The place is packed with cowboys
chasing Jim Beam with Olympia,
complaining about the tourists
they're sick of already,
though happy to drink off their money.

When a local lady says it's time,
she summons what grace she possesses
and follows her lead from bar stool to bar,
managing a precarious can-can
on the beer-slick mahogany.

The obliging bartender clears
her path of mugs and pitchers
with one clean sweep of his arm.
An Indian across the room
curses, chalks his cue
like it's her fault he scratched
on the eight ball.

Outside, a mountain man hangs
bare-assed from a neon fowl,
carrying on about whiskey
and women, and howling
at the stark Montana moon.

She Thinks She Smells a Bad Metaphor

For years she's worn nothing
but patchouly and musk,
rubbing the earthy oils
between her breasts, behind her ears,
into the crook of her arm
until the sweetness became her
signature, lingering
even in the books she has read.

But now she's overwhelmed
with gifts of fragrance:
Magie Noire from her mother
Intimate from her boss
White Linen from her widowed aunt
Woodhue from a man who knows she won't.

With so many scents to choose from
she's afraid she'll lose
her own, not recognize the trails
her body leaves her and be left
running round in circles, barking
up a tree that holds no game.

Even the faithful dog
she's fed for years will
sniff her crotch and whine
at the unfamiliar redolence of *Heaven Scent*
or *Charles of the Ritz*.

She knows she is no *Zanadu*.
No *Opium*. No *Obsession*.

At night her lover tells her
she's raw oysters
and honey. In the morning
she tastes *L'air du Temps* on his tongue.

For Her Villain

The time that she wastes missing him is hell,
though no one banks a fire that has grown cold.
And so she thinks she'll write this villanelle.

Though forms are frames she doesn't fit in well
she thinks that forcing pain into a mold
of verse might help free her from the hell

of missing him. If only she could tell
the truth from all the lies that have been told
and make sense of it in this villanelle,

her heart might open like a prison cell
and she might be released from the long hold
he's had on her. Not holding him is hell.

She tries to tell herself it's just as well.
That even if love could be bought and sold
it would cost him more than his cheap villanelle.

In this vignette, she plays the helpless Nell
tied to the tracks or stranded in the cold.
And like a dark-eyed demon straight from hell,
he plays the villain. Here's his villanelle.

She Changes Frogs

It is not always a kiss
that transforms him.
In fact, in one version
she has to knock him
up against a wall to achieve
the desired result.

Some point to her change of heart
and declare: *Another fickle woman!*
But his cold-blooded manner
would have forced the noblest love
to some strange end.

All that croaking
at the dinner table,
the swamp mud on her royal lap
and the slime in her canopied bed.
Not to mention her daddy, the king,
always lecturing her on promises,
as if he'd never broken
one himself.

Thus came the ever after day
when the princess
had to ask herself:
*is all this worth it
for just one golden ball?*

Her Happily Ever After

His father told him
Never trust a woman, son,
especially a pretty one.
So he never does

although he marries a girl
who is lovely, and true
as a woman can be to someone
other than herself.

He buys her a house he likes.
He doubts every word she speaks.
He tells a few lies of his own
just in case, or in spite.

She never complains or understands.
She tends a garden of herbs.
She works elaborate needlepoints
and cooks his favorite meals.

Years pass this way.
Small talk gives in to silence.
They age; her beauty fades.
Still he thinks she might prove false.

The warning hangs like a tapestry
between them; neither remembers
ever caring. Her stitches grow
finer and finer.
He drinks. No one recalls
their once upon a time.

The Men on Her Roof

She envies them for more
than agility or guts, the view
they're too busy to notice.

It's the fact that they begin
and end, are called upon
by folks like her who need

to keep their feet on firmer ground.
From where she pauses to watch
they appear lizard-like

scaling her walls on
their ladders, but she knows
they have a mission

they're sure to accomplish.
Some loose shingles or missing slate
will be back in place, the house secured

against the elements before they quit
and descend, while inside she trudges
her familiar terrain of rugs

and floors—Sisyphus with a vacuum
waging an endless war against her mountain
of proliferating dust. It's not so much

the doing as the fact it's never done
that makes a chore of necessary labor.
She knows ordinary lives need space

arranged for order and comfort.
But wonders if beds left unmade for a day
would keep anyone from dreaming?

If cobwebs beneath a love seat
would be a denial of love?
When the banging above her ceases

she trusts the men have done their work
well and hands them a check
for more than the estimate said

it was going to cost. They head off
to what she imagines—beer and burgers.
Smokes. A good game of pool.

And she resumes rearranging her den,
pushing the couch into a different
corner. She thinks it opens up

the room—makes it looks a little
larger—lets the potted palm
in its wicker cage take in
a little more light.

When in Doubt

No matter what happens, she pretends
she is used to such things.
Whatever comes off the wall
is no surprise to her.
Whatever comes through the door.

If her hands need something
to do with themselves,
she lights a cigarette.
No one seems to notice
if she doesn't exhale.

She tinkles the ice in her glass
if she has one. She rattles
her bracelets like bones.

With time, she settles
into the scene like dust
in corners, like furniture
not moved in years.

Wherever she happens
to find herself then
is as close as she gets to home.

She Has Days

she walks through wondering
what it would be like

to be someone, anyone
other than who she is:
the woman at the market

wheeling a cart piled
with Pampers and beer
the housewife in a blue

plaid dress bending
over a new bed
of geraniums, coaxing

color from poor soil
the hard-hatted woman
on Main Street behind

a MEN WORKING sign, stopping
the flow of traffic with a wave
of her strong, slender hand

the girl crouched on her porch swing
painting her toenails
pink—the very image

of concentration. It might
have something to do with
choices, but she can't recall

ever having chosen to be
what she is, where she's at
at this moment

only choosing to sleep
    late some mornings, to rise
        before dawn others—and even

this seemed more a force
    than choice, something urging
        her into or out of dreams

for no good reason, just to watch
    light play as it will across
        sky, through dust

on windows, choosing to wear
    one dress instead of another
        to turn left on the road

where a doe stands frightened
    transfixed by the lights of her car
        choosing to turn the lights off

and watch her shadow bound
    into a thicket, choosing
        to reply yes or no to a question

without thinking, and then
    having to live with the answer
        and think about why she ever

had to give it. But what does this
    have to do with today when the sky
        divides itself like a palette into shades

of gray it's hard not to see
    as a projection of her own
        mood, some split inside her

between darkness and another
   kind of darkness which lies
   just the other side of a light

strong enough to blind anyone
   who chooses to stare straight
     into it, squinting at the familiar

figure who wanders toward her
   in the market offering a choice
     piece of fruit, at the nursery

bearing seedlings in a plastic
   flat, wearing the sleek blue
     dress she decided to put on

this morning of her
   life on this green earth.

The Scholar

deconstructs *desire*, confines
it in language, which is,
he says, its element, the source
from which it flows.

On some level, she supposes,
he's right, but her mind
wearies from racing to
follow his train

of thought and collides
head-on with memory
in a tunnel called *love*
in a landscape called *pleasure*

and silence is the only
comment she can make fit him
inside her and breathless
in a darkness for which
there are no words to signify.

Demands of the Muse in Dreamtime

First-Chill-then Stupor-then the letting go

Emily Dickinson

Get back to writing
your life, he commands
as if this freeze could melt
and sweeten
her tongue into song.

There's too little *present*
she says, too much *past*.
She reminds him safety
costs cold—well, not
exactly cash—but . . .

He interrupts. *Excuses!*
Explanations, she insists.

But she begins to feel
everything she has been
x-ing out of experience.
And he knows he's got her.

Suddenly silence parts
like a curtain in an empty
hall onto a circle of
darkness that surrounds her.

She opens her mouth—an invitation.
He enters. A distant bird
she can't see or name starts
twittering a fragile *I*.

Notes

I. An Epic of the Eyes

The section title comes from Theodore Roethke's poem, *Open House.*

The titles *Large Bathers, Breakfast in Fur, Sky Cathedral,* and *Birthday* are taken from the art works to which they refer.

Though much of the raw material behind the poems comes from biographies, art history and critical texts, the contexts and conversations of the poems themselves are fictions.

II. Field Guide to the Ineffable

Marcel Duchamp: born 1887, Blainville, France. From 1915 until his death in 1968, he lived mostly in the United States. The Philadelphia Museum of Art houses one of the most complete collections of Duchamp's work in the world.

Marcel Dreams a Match with Paul Cezanne—Duchamp made several paintings of chess players (he was a master chess player and for many years more interested in chess than art). Among Cezanne's paintings are several of card players.

Readymades #1, 2 & 3 —Duchamp's most notorious works were his so-called "readymades," which included an inverted urinal titled *Fountain* (signed Richard Mutt) and a snow shovel titled *In Advance Of The Broken Arm.* He also created several works using chance procedures, such as dropping string onto a canvas. These poems were created choosing fragments of quotations from Duchamp at random. Literally, picking them out of a hat.

Marcel & Man Ray Play Tennis—the two really did play tennis the first time they met, at which point Duchamp spoke no English. They remained friends for life.

Sisters: Simultaneous—based on Duchamp's painting *Yvonne and Magdaleine in Tatters*

Rrose Sélavy No Longer Sings LA VIE EN ROSE—There is a famous portrait of Duchamp posed in drag (as Rrose) by Man Ray. Duchamp signed some of his works with Rrose's name, which is a pun on *c'est la vie*—and perhaps *eros c'est la vie*.

Song for a Sad Young Man—based on Duchamp's painting *Sad Young Man On A Train*. Duchamp composed a few works inspired by Laforgue.

Me & Marcel at the Five & Dime—Duchamp once said he planned to sign the Woolworth's building and make it the world's largest readymade.

The Joke on LA JOCONDE—in one of Duchamp's "assisted readymades", he drew a goatee and mustache on a postcard of the Mona Lisa (*La Joconde* in French) and titled it *L.H.O.O.Q.* When those letters are pronounced aloud, they sound like "elle a chaud au cul," which translates, "she has a hot ass." He said he thought she really looked like a man.

The Bride Not Even, Nor Her Bachelors Bare—based on Duchamp's *The Bride Stripped Bare By Her Bachelors, Even,* commonly referred to as *The Large Glass,* which was shattered while being moved and painstakingly reassembled.

Marcel Meets Georgia at 291—291 was Alfred Steiglitz's Gallery in New York.

Given: More Than Water & Gas—based on Duchamp's final work, *Etant donnes: 1. la chute d'eau 2. le gaz d'eclarage* (translation—*Given: 1. the waterfall 2. the illuminating gas*)

Several books informed the writing of these poems, including *Marcel Duchamp* by Sarane Alexandrian, *Marcel Duchamp in Perspective* edited by Joseph Mascheck, *Salt Seller: The Writings of Marcel Duchamp* edited by Michel Sanouillet and Elmer Peterson, and *Duchamp: A Biography* by Calvin Tomkins.

III. Where You've Seen Her

While this series of poems was *inspired*, as it were, by Cindy Sherman's self portraits (at least as I see them), the poems do not refer to any particular photographs.

Grace Bauer is the author of *The Women at the Well* (Portals Press, 1997), as well as three chapbooks of poems: *Where You've Seen Her* (Pennywhistle Press), *The House Where I've Never Lived* (Anabiosis Press), and *Field Guide to the Ineffable: Poems on Marcel Duchamp* (Snail's Pace Press). Her poems, stories, and essays have appeared in numerous anthologies and journals, including: *Arts & Letters, Colorado Review, Doubletake, Margie, Poetry, Rattle, Southern Poetry Review,* and others. She is co-editor (with Julie Kane) of the anthology, *Umpteen Ways of Looking at A Possum: Creative And Critical Responses to Everette Maddox* (Xavier Review Press). She teaches at the University of Nebraska-Lincoln.